The Disinformation Dance: Understanding and Confronting Propaganda

Table of Content

CHAPTER 7: PROTECTING DEMOCRACY IN THE INFORMATION AGE49

CONCLUSION: RECLAIMING REALITY 59

ABOUT THE AUTHOR 61

Introduction

We live in an age overwhelmed by information. News, ideas, and messages bombard us 24/7 through television, radio, the internet, and smartphones. While access to information was once scarce, today many of us feel lost in a never-ending flood of content.

But more than the sheer volume of information, what defines our time is the massive proliferation of MISINFORMATION: claims that are false or misleading, yet spread rapidly thanks to digital media. Of all forms of misinformation, propaganda and disinformation aimed at manipulating public opinion are the most dangerous. Partisan fake news, deepfakes, viral conspiracy theories, misattributed quotes, and state-sponsored cyberwarfare are just a few of the ways that truth is twisted and warped today.

This book focuses on one vital question: how can citizens like you and me avoid being duped and make sense of reality in the modern world? I don't assert that I have all the answers. But as a psychologist who has studied propaganda and media literacy over the years, I've picked up some techniques that we all can use. This book aims to equip you with essential knowledge and critical thinking skills to detect propaganda, fact-check claims, and confront the "disinformation dance" we are faced with daily.

In the following chapters, we'll cover:

- What exactly propaganda is and how it differs from misinformation and disinformation. We'll look at the specific techniques used to manipulate opinions, emotions, and behavior.

- Fascinating historical examples of propaganda campaigns through the ages. Understanding how propaganda has evolved over time provides important context for spotting it today.

- An in-depth examination of propaganda's modern-day breeding grounds on social media, partisan cable news, conspiracy theory websites, and beyond. We'll look at how

algorithms, advertising dollars, and psychology fuel
misinformation across the political spectrum.

- Step-by-step tools you can use to fact-check claims, analyze
media bias, verify sources, and detect the logical flaws and
emotional manipulation that underlie propaganda. I'll share
the same skills we teach our students in media literacy
courses.

- Ways you can personally build resilience against propaganda
by diversifying your information diet, connecting with
quality journalism, and strengthening critical thinking. We'll
also explore grassroots community responses.

- Policy and technology reforms that could help mitigate
propaganda's spread. I'll share innovative solutions that
preserve free speech while combating disinformation. Media
literacy education is key.

Equipped with a deeper understanding of the modern propaganda
landscape, you'll be able to navigate news and social media with
savvier eyes. Instead of just consuming information, you'll be
empowered to analyze, question, verify, and respond.

The issues explored in this book affect all citizens who care about
engaging with reality, rejecting falsehoods, and protecting
democracy. I don't aim to tell you what to believe, only to provide
tools to help you shape your own informed opinions. With vigilance
and critical thinking, we can keep spinning with truth as our partner.

Chapter 1: What is Propaganda?

Before we can counter propaganda, we need to clearly define what it is and how it operates. This chapter will break down key terminology and give an overview of common propaganda techniques used to distort the truth.

Defining Propaganda

Merriam-Webster dictionary defines propaganda as:

"The spreading of ideas, information, or rumor for the purpose of helping or injuring an institution, a cause, or a person."

The key point is that propaganda is communication designed to manipulate people's beliefs and actions. Unlike objective information, it aims to promote a biased agenda.

Propaganda often has negative connotations thanks to its use in totalitarian states. But it can promote any cause or viewpoint - good or bad. Whether it's a health campaign against smoking or a dictator's cult of personality, PERSUASIVE MESSAGING THAT SKEWS FACTS TO PROMOTE ONE SIDE is propaganda.

How Propaganda Differs from Misinformation and Disinformation

Propaganda overlaps with two other problematic types of information: misinformation and disinformation.

- **Misinformation** is false or inaccurate information that is spread mistakenly without malicious intent. For example, a person might honestly share a false news story on social media believing it to be true. Misinformation can be spread by anyone.

- **Disinformation**, on the other hand, is intentionally being deceptive. Disinformation is false information that is knowingly spread to deceive the public, obscure facts, or cause harm. For instance, a dictator might plant made-up stories to discredit political rivals. Disinformation is spread with malicious intent.

Propaganda can include elements of both misinformation and disinformation. Propaganda often uses lies, exaggerations, and misleading claims to promote a biased agenda. However, propaganda has a broader scope beyond just false information.

Attributes of Propaganda

While propaganda can take limitless forms, most exhibits these traits:

- Has a clear bias or agenda

- Uses selective, distorted, or fabricated information

- Appeals to emotions rather than intellect

- Oversimplifies complex issues

- Demonizes opposition and critics

- Repeats big lies and memorable slogans

Skilled propagandists tailor their messages to be convincing based on the target audience's fears, values, and beliefs. Propaganda tells people what they want to hear rather than presenting reality.

Next, we'll overview classic propaganda techniques used to control narratives. Being aware of these tricks is key to recognizing propaganda in action.

Common Propaganda Techniques

1. Bandwagon Effect

This technique encourages people to align with the majority, follow trends, and avoid standing out. Propagandists present an idea as fashionable, new, or cutting-edge to get people to adopt it. Or they claim "everyone is doing it" to pressure acceptance.

Examples:

- "All the fashionable youngsters are sporting these trendy shoes."

- "Every patriot supports this policy. Do you?"

2. Glittering Generalities

This uses vague, broad, positive language to play on emotions and build acceptance for an idea. Words like freedom, honor, liberty, or justice have positive associations but fuzzy meanings that can be twisted to justify anything.

Examples:

- "Our glorious nation will forever stand as a beacon of freedom."

- "Elect me to bring back prosperity and family values."

3. Lesser of Two Evils

This limits choices to two bad options, fooling you into picking the less-bad one that the propagandist actually prefers. It frames the propagandist's goal as the least-worst option.

Examples:

- "Grant us the authority to collect your data, or else, be ready for an increase in terrorism."

- "While this plan may have its flaws, the alternative is nothing short of disastrous."

4. Name Calling

This technique demonizes opponents by calling them names that evoke negative emotions. If you associate something or someone with bad qualities, you're more likely to reject them.

Examples:

- Referring to a political candidate as "Crooked Hillary" or "Crazy Bernie."

- Calling political opponents traitors, radicals, evil, etc.

5. Pinpointing the Enemy

This identifies a specific person, group, or nation as an enemy threat. Doing so rallies people against a common enemy and diverts blame. Scapegoating is a frequent propaganda tactic.

Examples:

- "Immigrants are having an adverse effect on our economy and taking away job opportunities from you."

- "The Russians are hacking our democracy."

6. Plain Folks

Here a leader pretends to be just like regular people to build broad appeal. Despite wealth or high status, they present themselves as ordinary folks you can relate to and trust.

Examples:

- A billionaire politician emphasizing his simple, small-town roots.

- A pop star discussing her humble background and money struggles.

7. Repetition

No propaganda technique is more effective than simple repetition. If you repeat any idea often enough, people will eventually accept it. A big lie stated frequently becomes true in people's minds.

Examples:

- A repeated campaign slogan like "Yes We Can."

- Frequently blurting out the same keyword or phrase.

8. Transfer (or Guilt/Virtue by Association)

This technique transfers the positive or negative qualities of something or someone to another by association. It links two unrelated things to transfer feelings about one onto the other.

Examples:

- Displaying a politician with patriotic symbols like flags to paint them as patriotic.

- Photographing a celebrity using a certain product to transfer positive feelings to that brand.

9. Unproven Claims

Propaganda often makes dramatic assertions without any evidence or proof. These claims play on fears, spread conspiracy theories, or promise incredible benefits if the propagandist gets their way.

Examples:

- "Our society is spiraling into chaos devoid of any structure."

- "Elect me and I'll lower taxes, create jobs, and restore world peace."

In Review

Identifying propaganda starts with recognizing its goal to selectively manipulate opinion. While propaganda twists the truth, simply being biased, misleading, or emotional does not necessarily make something propaganda. We now have a solid foundation to build skills for detecting and analyzing propaganda in the chapters ahead.

The disinformation dance is centuries old, but social media provides new fertile ground for propaganda to thrive - as we'll explore next.

Chapter 2: A Brief History of Propaganda

Propaganda has played a central role in politics, war, religion, and power struggles across human history. In this chapter, we'll explore the evolution of propaganda and disinformation tactics from ancient times up through the internet age. Understanding historical context shines a light on how and why propaganda works.

Early Origins of Persuasion and Propaganda

The deliberate use of information to manipulate public opinion stretches back thousands of years. Some of the earliest examples come from ancient Roman and Chinese civilizations.

Ancient Rome

In ancient Rome, political rivals competed for popular support using paid announcements called PROCLAMATIONES. These were posted in public places and often contained image-crafting propaganda about a leader's accomplishments.

Roman emperors also used propaganda for succession and control. When Augustus Caesar rose to power around 27 BCE, he launched massive propaganda campaigns. These promoted him as the divine savior who had brought peace to Rome after years of civil war.

Ancient China

The ancient Chinese philosopher and strategist Sun Tzu wrote about wartime psychological operations and misinformation in his famous book THE ART OF WAR around 500 BCE:

"All warfare is based on deception. Hence, when we are able to attack, we must seem unable; when using our forces, we must appear inactive."—Sun Tzu

In ancient Chinese warfare, military generals actively spread rumors and misinformation to deceive rival states.

Propaganda was a key tool for empires to wield control and project power from the earliest civilizations. Next, we'll see how propaganda evolved in the 20th century's world wars.

Propaganda in World War I and World War II

The violent nationalism and mass mechanized warfare of the World Wars took propaganda to unprecedented extremes. Governments professionally weaponized propaganda to mobilize civilian populations.

World War I

During World War I, professional propaganda offices formed on all sides of the conflict.

The British propaganda bureau circulated outrageous fake stories about German "corpse factories" where bodies of dead soldiers were allegedly converted into chemicals and animal feed. This aimed to turn public opinion against Germany.

America's Committee of Public Information exaggerated German atrocities with fabricated stories like soldiers bayonetting babies and crucifying women. They urged Americans to "make the world safe for democracy" and defeat the barbaric Germans.

World War II

Propaganda played an even bigger role in World War II, aided by new mass media like radio and film.

Nazi Germany stands as history's most chilling example of state propaganda. Joseph Goebbels headed Nazi propaganda efforts, systematically indoctrinating Germans through education, media control, and destroying opposing voices.

Hitler and Goebbels used repetition of simple slogans, censorship, fearmongering, and scapegoating of Jews to turn Germans to fascism. Controlling all communication channels allowed the Nazis to rapidly spread disinformation and turn fiction into "truth" through continual repetition.

All sides used propaganda in World War II, but Nazi propaganda remains the textbook case of how concerted propaganda can utterly reshape a society based on lies and irrational hatred.

The Cold War and KGB Disinformation

Even after World War II, propaganda shaped geopolitics during the Cold War between capitalist and communist states.

The Soviet Union's intelligence agency KGB engaged in active "disinformation" operations against the West. They deliberately spread false information to sow confusion and turn public opinion against enemies.

A classic example is "Operation INFEKTION," a disinformation campaign launched in the 1980s to convince the world that the CIA created AIDS. The KGB fabricated a letter purporting to prove CIA scientists developed AIDS as a biological weapon. This baseless claim went viral globally and the conspiracy theory persists today.

Through Cold War propaganda, both the Soviet Union and United States vied for geopolitical dominance and demonized each other as mortal enemies. Propaganda was a constant companion of military power and international relations.

Propaganda in the Digital Age

The internet and social media have transformed propaganda's scale and potential like nothing before. Some even say we've entered an "post-truth" era of politics. Next, we'll overview how modern technology has aided the disinformation dance.

Characteristics of Online Propaganda

Digital networks allow propaganda to rapidly spread and micro-target specific demographics. Key traits make online propaganda uniquely troubling:

- **Virality** - Disinformation can "go viral" globally in hours through shares and posts. Rumors spread like wildfire.

- **Anonymity** - Agents can disguise identities and origins to stealthily spread propaganda. Bots and fake accounts abound.

- **Microtargeting** - Data collection aids precision propaganda focused on specific groups' biases.

- **Selective Exposure** - People tend to consume media that confirms their existing views, creating echo chambers.

- **Algorithmic Amplification** - Sites like Facebook may highlight more "engaging" (outrageous) content in feeds, inadvertently boosting propaganda.

- **Deepfakes** - AI can generate fake images, videos, and text that look real, making fabricated propaganda easier than ever.

These modern conditions allow propaganda to spread at an unprecedented scale. Next, we'll look at some tactics used by states to manipulate online discourse.

Cyberwarfare and State-Sponsored Propaganda

Nation states now regularly use propaganda cyberwarfare to advance agendas abroad. This involves hacking, strategic leaks, and social media influence operations. For instance:

- **Russia** - Used networks of fake accounts and automated bots to spread disinformation and sow division in the West during elections. Strategic hacks and email leaks also aimed to tilt political outcomes.

- **China** - Employs a massive online propaganda apparatus to censor dissent and spread state messaging abroad, including the "50 Cent Army" of social media commentators.

- **North Korea** - Runs online influence operations to spread regime propaganda and misinformation demonizing the West.

- **Iran** - Uses "sock puppet" accounts to pose as locals and steer discussions in various countries to promote Iranian interests.

Such state-sponsored propaganda represents a new form of cyber warfare to shape narratives and public opinion in rival nations. Governments are top players in the disinformation game.

Characteristics of Modern Propaganda Campaigns

While their techniques constantly evolve, most modern propaganda campaigns have certain elements:

- **Mixes truth with lies** - Blatant "fake news" is less common than distortions of real events and selective facts that paint one-sided narratives.

- **Exploits tensions** - Propaganda often amplifies societal divides around issues like race, immigration, and religion to stir conflict.

- **Vilifies opponents** - Those with contrasting views are painted as evil, corrupt enemies. Opposing facts are explained away as liars' conspiracies.

- **Uses influential nodes** - Propaganda spreads efficiently by influencing media personalities, political figures, and "influencers" with large networks to repeat and lend credibility to messages.

- **Obscures origins** - Modern propaganda hides and denies its coordination to seem organic. But trace it back and you often find a central organization pulling strings behind the curtain.

Recognizing these common tactics helps reveal when a persuasive message aims to manipulate rather than inform.

Lessons from the Past

With historical context, we can clearly see how propaganda relates to power. Those in power or seeking power used propaganda and censorship to control narratives that solidified their rule.

Propaganda exploits human biases: our tribal tendencies, cognitive shortcuts, and emotions like hope, fear, and anger. Skilled propagandists bend these innate weaknesses to their benefit rather than appealing to reason.

Robust propaganda impacts not just individuals, but entire societies - as the Nazi case horrifically proved. When reality gets defined top-down by those controlling communications, the consequence can be mass delusion and atrocity.

Can we ordinary citizens counter such orchestrated efforts to hack human psychology in the digital age? I believe so, armed with knowledge of how propaganda operates. The disinformation dance adapts to new technologies, but ancient techniques live on. In coming chapters, we'll build skills for cutting through propaganda in the modern world.

Chapter 3: How Propaganda Spreads Today

The digital age provides endless channels for propaganda and misinformation to spread and target specific groups. In this chapter, we'll dive into the modern breeding grounds for disinformation across social media, partisan cable news, conspiracy sites, and more.

Understanding how these ecosystems work illuminates why propaganda thrives today. We'll also debunk some common myths about the online disinformation crisis.

Social Media and "Fake News"

Social media platforms like Facebook, Twitter, and YouTube have transformed how billions consume news and information. Their powerful algorithms, selective exposure, and rapid sharing allow propaganda to spread like wildfire.

Virality Fuels Disinformation

On social platforms, engagement drives visibility. Content that elicits strong emotions - outrage, shock, fear - tends to be shared more often than balanced, nuanced stories. This creates an environment where sensationalized, one-sided propaganda goes viral.

MIT researchers analyzed over 10 million Twitter shares of mainstream and fake news stories in 2016 and 2017. They found false news travelled SIX TIMES FASTER than accurate news - the most viral fakes reached over 100,000 people compared to the truth rarely reaching 10,000. Lies spread faster than facts on social networks.

Algorithms Amplify Propaganda

Social media platforms use complex, secretive algorithms to determine what content users see in newsfeeds or search results.

These automated systems analyze your interests based on past activity to recommend personalized content.

However, in doing so, algorithms often unintentionally AMPLIFY disinformation. By prioritizing "engaging" posts with strong emotions and reactions, algorithms boost inflammatory propaganda that gets people riled up. Systems designed for relevance and retention gravitate toward misinformation.

Social Bots and Inauthentic Accounts

Online propaganda efforts often involve networks of fake accounts, also called "bots," that artificially boost disinformation. These inauthentic accounts impersonate real users to automatically post content or engage with other accounts.

Researchers estimate 10-15% of Twitter accounts are likely bots. Such networks allow nearly any message to start trending and appear to go viral. Paid "troll farms" abuse bots on an industrial scale to artificially manipulate social discourse.

Microtargeting Vulnerable Groups

Advanced data analytics and tracking allow social media ads and posts to precisely target users with certain demographics and interests. This means propaganda can be customized to exploit the biases of specific groups prone to conspiracy theories or other vulnerable narratives.

For example, Cambridge Analytica notoriously used psychographic targeting in the 2016 US election to influence voters based on personality profiles. Such microtargeting enhances the effectiveness of online propaganda.

Cable News and Political Propaganda

Cable television revolutionized American news media over the past three decades by introducing 24/7 partisan opinion programming on channels like Fox News and MSNBC. This polarized "infotainment" provides fertile ground for political propaganda.

The Rise of Subjective Punditry

In cable news today, traditional objective reporting has taken a backseat to partisan commentary by pundits defending their side. Channels like Fox News feature lineups stacked with right-wing personalities who spin news to fit conservative narratives. MSNBC leverages left-leaning hosts in similar fashion.

This blurring of news and subjective opinion creates an environment ripe for propaganda. Reporting gives way to politically-skewed narratives aimed more at keeping viewers outraged and engaged than informing them accurately.

Demonizing the "Other Side"

A common propaganda tactic used by partisan cable channels is relentlessly attacking and demonizing the opposing party. For example, certain Fox News figures constantly hype the idea that Democrats are radical socialist destroyers of American values. MSNBC personalities similarly portray Trump supporters as racist extremists.

This good vs. evil framing divides America into warring tribes and breeds distrust, anger, and misperceptions about fellow citizens on the "other side." It also rallies audiences to support one's own party at any cost.

Echo Chambers and Radicalization

The tribal structure of cable news fosters "echo chambers" where viewers hear only voices from their own political tribe while other perspectives go unheard. Being exposed solely to biased takes from one's own "team" leads audiences to become more radicalized in their views over time - particularly on emotionally-charged issues like race and immigration.

The propaganda narratives promoted in such echo chambers quickly become "truth" for audiences denied exposure to alternate analysis. This extreme tunnel vision fuels America's partisan divides. Audiences often accept even questionable claims if they confirm pre-existing biases.

Conspiracy Theory Websites and Forums

The internet also enables once-fringe conspiracy theories to gain huge audiences through dedicated sites and online communities. These ecosystems actively generate and spread disinformation targeting those prone to conspiratorial thinking.

Exploiting Biases

Certain personality traits and cognitive biases make some people more receptive to conspiracy theories, which attribute societal problems or events to secret elite plots. These include:

- Desire for understanding complex events

- Distrust of authority figures

- Feelings of powerlessness or social isolation

- Black-and-white thinking

Sites like Infowars and message boards like 4chan/pol/ leverage these mental shortcuts and vulnerabilities to hook audiences seeking forbidden "truths."

Manufacturing Faux Evidence

One common tactic used by conspiracy sites is fabricating complex webs of "evidence" to back their claims. For example, elaborate visual charts supposedly connecting various world leaders and events to prove a globalist plot. Even if each individual claim is questionable, the overall breadth makes it seem well-supported for those inclined to believe.

Conspiracy theorists also cherry-pick and misrepresent legitimate info, research, and news reports to artificially validate their narratives. These propaganda techniques manufacture an illusion of credibility.

Trolling and Harassment

Many online conspiracy and extremist communities urge real-world harassment of perceived enemies and skeptics of the conspiracy narrative. Members "investigate" targets, reveal personal details, and coordinate campaigns of abuse - a toxic blend of propaganda, radicalization, and vigilante trolling.

In some cases this escalates to extreme violence against demonized scapegoats. The Pizzagate conspiracy led to a shooter firing an AR-15 in a Washington D.C. restaurant. Rampant Islamophobic propaganda contributes to hate crimes against Muslims. Online radicalization has real-world consequences.

State-Sponsored Troll Farms

Certain governments now sponsor dedicated propaganda units that covertly operate from offices disguised as commercial entities to create an illusion of organic activity. These carry out large-scale trolling and disinformation campaigns on social media.

Russia's Internet Research Agency

The most infamous example is Russia's Internet Research Agency, also known as Glavset. This organization in St. Petersburg employs hundreds of workers to pose as locals online and spread pro-Russia propaganda in many languages targeting foreign nations.

They create fake accounts across social networks, forums, and comments sections - hijacking hashtags and steering conversations to sow discord, distrust institutions, boost Russian interests, and inflame societal tensions. Such centrally-run national propaganda represents a new form of information warfare.

China's 50 Cent Army

China similarly employs a covert online propaganda apparatus nicknamed the "50 Cent Army." These paid commenters get nickels for each social media post defending the Communist Party, promoting its image, and criticizing opponents.

They swarm domestic sites like Weibo to censor dissent. Internationally, they spread state messaging on Twitter and YouTube (both banned in China). Leaked records in 2014 identified over 300 50 Cent Army accounts - and the real total likely numbers in the hundreds of thousands.

Obscuring Origins

Unlike independent organic trolls, state troll farms disguise their origins and coordination, posing as regular users. They exhibit lingual and cultural knowledge of target countries to better manipulate foreign discourse and seem local.

As propaganda tools, such troll armies allow authoritarian regimes to project strategic power abroad. Their online warfare aims to demoralize enemies and fracture Western unity.

Trends and Tactics in Modern Propaganda

This overview highlights how modern media ecosystems enable propaganda, misinformation, and extremism to spread and thrive. However, the online disinformation crisis stems from complex dynamics with no single cause. Next we'll explore four key factors that interact to determine propaganda's potency.

1. Media Business Models and Incentives

Digital advertising dollars have crippled journalism. Clicks and outrage drive profits. Objective reporters are laid off while pundits playing to biases thrive. Regulation could help reform media business models to reduce financial incentives for misinformation.

2. Sophisticated Propagandists

Skilled manipulators adept at propaganda tactics and social psychology intentionally create and spread disinformation for power and profit. Understanding their methods is crucial.

3. Algorithmic Amplification

As discussed, platforms' AI systems unintentionally boost inflammatory content through recommending what's engaging. Improved algorithms and human oversight may reduce this issue.

4. Public Resonance and Appetite

Propaganda only spreads when people choose to view, like, and share it - it resonates by appealing to human biases. So solutions require examining our own vulnerabilities. Media literacy education can immunize the public.

In summary, modern systems amplify human weaknesses and allow organized propagandists to exploit them at scale. But recognizing how this ecosystem enables the disinformation crisis points toward solutions we'll discuss later. First, we need to build skills for detecting and analyzing propaganda claims.

Chapter 4: Detecting Propaganda and Misinformation

Now equipped with a solid grasp of common propaganda techniques and the modern misinformation landscape, we'll shift gears to exploring practical skills for recognizing these tactics in the wild.

This chapter provides specific methods anyone can use to critically analyze claims, fact-check information, identify falsehoods and misrepresentations, evaluate media bias, and cut through manipulation strategies. Mastering this analytical toolkit is power.

Developing Your Propaganda Radar

The first line of defense against propaganda is cultivating an initial skepticism whenever you encounter a persuasive claim or narrative. Simply ask yourself:

- Who is spreading this message and what is their agenda?

- What are they trying to make me feel or do?

- Is this solely factual or does it aim to manipulate?

Approaching information this way activates your propaganda "radar" to identify attempts at manipulation even if specific techniques aren't yet visible.

Before accepting a claim, first pause to reflect on the communicator's goals rather than just reacting. This buys time for the rational mind to engage. Now let's examine specific methods for analyzing content.

Technique 1: Fact-Checking Claims

In an era where technology makes fabricating any claim easy, fact-checking remains crucial. When evaluating a statement:

- **Check primary sources** - Find and review the original source being cited rather than relying on someone else's interpretation. For example, read the entire original research paper or documentary footage if available.

- **Verify key details** - Check whether names, dates, times, statistics, quotes, documents, images etc. mentioned can be corroborated from reputable independent sources. Propagandists often base lies around a shred of truth.

- **Research the source** - Analyze who is behind the claim and their credibility on this topic. Are they an expert or authoritative figure? Do they have a history of accuracy and honesty? Or do they have a clear bias, agenda, or incentive to spread misinformation?

- **Look for consistency** - Review if other fact-checkers and credible sources corroborate the claim or conflict with it. Lies often crumble when scrutinized from multiple angles.

- **Ask experts** - For complex issues, consult independent experts qualified to judge the claim's validity based on scientific consensus or available evidence in their field.

Using these methods to independently verify claims rather than passively accepting them immunizes you against propaganda falsehoods.

Technique 2: Evaluating Sources

When analyzing an article, video, social media post, or other content, it's critical to evaluate the credibility of the source.

- **Look for transparency** - Reputable sources provide names of creators, contact info, disclosure of ownership, and clearly display corrections. Anonymous or vague sources warrant skepticism.

- **Research author expertise** - Highly qualified authors with subject matter credentials and a track record of impartial analysis tend to be more credible. Clickbait content farms, however, hire amateur freelancers to churn out articles.

- **Note citations** - Credible reporting cites multiple independent sources and original data. Lack of links, footnotes, or mentions of how info was gathered reveals weaker sourcing.

- **Consider potential bias** - What is the source's political leaning, conflicts of interest, or incentives that could introduce bias? Extreme partisan sources warrant caution.

- **Verify other claims** - Scan other articles by the source. Do these demonstrate accuracy, reasoned analysis, and adherence to facts? Or promote sensationalism, conspiracy theories, and unproven claims?

Evaluating sources helps determine which warrant your trust versus healthy skepticism.

Technique 3: Identifying Logical Fallacies

Logical fallacies are flaws in reasoning that undermine an argument's validity. Learning to spot them reveals when a claim seeks to manipulate rather than convince rationally. Common fallacies to watch for include:

False Dilemma - Presenting only two extreme options when others exist. Example: " We must either undertake this or face a disastrous outcome."

Ad Hominem Attack - Attacking someone's character rather than addressing their argument. Example: " Ignore him, he can't be relied upon."

Straw Man Argument - Misrepresenting someone's position to easily knock it down. Example: "Are you suggesting that you desire disorder and lawlessness?"

Slippery Slope Argument - Claiming one small step will inevitably lead to an extreme outcome without justification. Example: " If we allow this to happen, they will gradually deprive us of all our rights and benefits."

Cherry Picking - Highlighting only information that confirms one's position while ignoring contrary evidence.

Bandwagon Appeal - Attempting to win support for an idea by claiming "everyone's doing it."

Learning to recognize these and other fallacies takes practice, but soon you'll notice them constantly in propaganda.

Technique 4: Analyzing Word Choices and Framing

The specific words and phrasing used to communicate an idea also matter hugely. Skilled propagandists construct linguistic frames to subtly influence audiences.

When interpreting a message, pay attention to:

- **Loaded words** - Language that triggers emotional reactions. Example: saying a politician "attacked" versus "criticized" a policy.

- **Labeling** - Applying simplistic terms or categories that prime audience reactions. Examples: "radical," "conspiracy theorist," "socialist."

- **Euphemisms** - Using inoffensive words that mask ugly realities. Example: saying "enhanced interrogation" instead of "torture."

- **Exaggeration** - Over-the-top phrasing that distorts reality. Example: "They're gutting the whole Constitution."

- **Missing Context** - Framing a true statement in a misleading way by omitting key details.

- **False Implications** - Creating suggestive statements that lead audiences to fill in false inferences.

Analyzing word choices reveals how language frames narratives, downplaying negative traits on one's own side while exaggerating them on the opposing side.

Technique 5: Identifying Emotional Manipulation

Skillful propaganda triggers emotions like fear, anger, or outrage rather than appealing to reason. When encountering strong emotional language, stop and ask yourself:

- **What feelings is this content trying to stoke in me?** Outrage? Hate? Fear? Disgust? Excitement?

- **Are graphic visuals or descriptions aimed to shock or scare?**

- **What action does it want me to take as a result of these feelings?** Who does it want me to turn against? What should I now support or oppose?

Noticing emotional manipulation helps prevent instinctive reactions. Channel feelings into fuel for deeper investigation rather than blind acceptance.

Technique 6: Analyzing Images and Videos

Visual propaganda requires specialized skills to decode. When analyzing images and video:

- **Do reverse image searches** - Propagandists often mislabel or reuse existing unrelated images to illustrate fake stories. Searching Google Images or TinEye using an image's URL can reveal its earlier contexts if misappropriated.

- **Look for image tampering** - Photos may be doctored, edited, or altered from their original version. Forensic tools can detect fake details.

- **Check the source** - Is the photo or video attributed to a credible journalist or organization present at the event depicted? Or an anonymous social media account?

- **Confirm the date** - Google Maps, weather reports, and historical data can verify if images match the alleged date, time, and place.

- **Watch for missing context** - Images often capture fragments of a scene but exclude the full picture. Consider what occurred beyond the camera frame.

- **Beware cheap-fakes** - Simple editing like cropping, selective footage, or mislabeling can readily misrepresent reality. Altered audio tracks also deceive.

With critical analysis, propaganda imagery can speak truths that reveal a different reality from what the captions claim.

Technique 7: Evaluating "Journalism"

When assessing an article, report, documentary, or other journalism, gauge how well it adheres to traditional standards:

- **Neutral tone** - Reports facts without loaded language designed to provoke emotions or color interpretations.

- **Multiple cited sources** - Facts contain links to original sources or interviews with on-the-ground experts. Anonymous sourcing is limited and explained.

- **Original investigation** - Presents new findings from documents and data or the reporters' own eyewitness experience. Makes clear what is original versus aggregating others' existing reporting.

- **Provides context** - Situates facts within nuanced background to convey a complete narrative, rather than cherry-picking points out of context.

- **Transparent corrections** - Corrects errors by prominently noting details of corrections. Lack of needed correction suggests neglect for accuracy.

Journalism that abides by these long-standing standards demonstrates an intent to inform rather than mislead.

Technique 8: Tracking Propaganda Narratives

Focusing solely on debunking individual fake stories misses the cumulative influence of propaganda narratives. Try this:

- **Identify central themes** - Note common narratives repeated across sources and social networks. Certain ideas act as pillars for an overall worldview.

- **Trace origins** - Study how and where specific stories and frames originated and spread. Ongoing rumors often have notable "patient zeros."

- **Follow collaborators** - See which sources actively collaborate to reinforce the same narratives through linking, reposting, and collaborating.

- **Spot inconsistencies** - Track whether sources adjust narratives when the original version is disproven. Consistent evolution reveals coordination.

Methodically tracking flow and shifts in narratives over time unveils broader propaganda ecosystems.

Technique 9: Considering Commercial Incentives

Ask yourself: Who profits from this information or narrative? And how might that shape content?

- **Ads** - What sponsors or paid promoted content appear alongside or within reporting? And does this create conflicts of interest?

- **Audience targeting** - Is content designed to resonate with specific demographics valued by advertisers? Or to maximize engagement and sharing generally?

- **Organization ownership** - Who controls the outlet? Are they beholden to shareholders, venture capital investors, or private interest groups with their own agendas?

While platforms profit from engagement, users pay with time and attention. Remember you are the product.

Technique 10: Seeking Diverse Perspectives

Balancing perspectives dilutes potential bias and manipulation. Make an effort to:

- **Diversify sources** - Don't rely solely on one media ecosystem for information. Expose yourself to outlets across geographic regions, political leanings, and cultural communities.

- **Avoid echo chambers** - Following a narrow subset of perspectives on social media can warp perceptions. Actively seek alternate voices and analysis.

- **Change positions** - Entertain opposing views and play "devil's advocate" thought experiments. Imagine if you believed differently to grasp other angles.

- **Talk to real people** - Have genuine conversations face-to-face. The internet fails to convey nuance and humanity across lines of division.

Propaganda exploits tunnel vision. Proactively broadening inputs defends against insular radicalization and manipulation.

Conclusion

Mastering this analytical toolkit empowers citizens to cut through propaganda, disinformation, and manipulation. When skillfully investigating claims and evaluating sources rather than passively absorbing narratives, we regain agency over our own understanding of reality.

Wielding these critical thinking abilities, we are harder to fool and control. We can extract truth from torrents of propaganda.

In the next chapter, we'll shift to exploring how each of us can personally build resistance to propaganda's influence starting with our own minds. Because beyond analyzing propaganda strategically, we must also overcome our own vulnerabilities that allow disinformation to resonate in the first place.

Chapter 5: Inoculating Yourself Against Propaganda

The analytical skills we've built form the foundation for identifying and breaking down propaganda. But resisting propaganda's influence requires more than just fact-checking claims and detecting techniques.

We must go deeper to explore our own psychological vulnerabilities that allow disinformation to exploit emotions and manipulate behavior. This chapter focuses on building individual resilience against propaganda's influence starting with our perceptions and mental habits.

Propaganda is only dangerous when internalized. So strengthening our own defenses is crucial - we must become propaganda-proof. The strategies below help develop "mental immunity."

Cultivating Awareness

The first step to resisting propaganda's power is cultivating constant awareness of how it operates. Maintain heightened sensitivity by asking yourself:

- **What are the propagandist's goals here?** To provoke certain emotions? To get me to take certain actions? To see events through a specific narrative lens?

- **What techniques do I notice being used?** Loaded words, stereotyping, bandwagon pressure, fearmongering, misleading imagery etc. Become adept at recognizing specific tactics in real time.

- **How is it trying to manipulate me?** Through appealing to emotion rather than logic? Demonizing a scapegoat? Pressuring acceptance through repetition?

- **How am I reacting internally?** Do I notice strong feelings of outrage, fear, intimidation, or tribal loyalty emerging - emotions that hinder thoughtful processing?

Propaganda loses power once its mechanisms are seen rather than operating subconsciously. Staying aware puts you back in the driver's seat.

Prioritizing Critical Thinking

Also make critical thinking a habit, not just when examining questionable claims. Practice:

- **Asking probing questions** - Dig deeper by asking who, what, where, when, why, and how regarding any assertion or narrative. Query assumptions behind statements. Imagine counterarguments.

- **Evaluating evidence** - Insist any claim be backed by sufficient impartial proof that stands up to scrutiny from multiple angles. Withhold quick judgement without thorough investigation.

- **Seeking nuance** - Train yourself to catch absolutist, black-and-white thinking, and instead look for shades of grey. Truth often lies between extremes. Reject oversimplification.

- **Contemplating alternative views** - Entertain competing perspectives in depth, even on issues you feel strongly about. Don't just attack opposing views - understand them first, then identify flaws or agree with valid points.

Regularly engaging in critical thinking makes your brain more propaganda-resistant long-term. It cultivates tendencies that render you a less vulnerable target.

Diversifying Inputs

Propaganda thrives when we filter inputs to only those that confirm our existing views. Make media diversity a priority:

- **Vet sources rigorously** - Don't rely on outlets just because they reinforce your opinions. Check credibility indicators like those listed in Chapter 4 before trusting a source.

- **Venture beyond your bubble** - Follow figures with different ideologies and backgrounds. Seek content and viewpoints that challenge your beliefs. Discomfort leads to growth.

- **Limit echo chambers** - Be cautious of tight-knit social media communities united around a single viewpoint. While bonding, they often breed extremism and detachment from reality.

- **Sample broadly** - Proactively expose yourself to media produced for geographic and cultural communities distinct from your own.

Welcoming diverse inputs inoculates you against narrow indoctrination and balances biases, strengthening your immunity to targeted propaganda.

Evaluating Your Own Biases

We all absorb societal prejudices and cognitive blindspots that render us vulnerable to manipulation. Honestly inventory your own biases:

- **Note knee-jerk reactions** - Observe what topics, groups, or ideas immediately provoke hostility or alignment for you. Reaction speed denotes bias.

- **Question assumptions** - Scrutinize what default narratives or explanations you accept without evidence. Challenge why you believe them.

- **Watch for hypocrisy** - Do you judge the same behaviors differently depending on the group? Are you quicker to criticize those you see as opponents? Double standards reveal bias.

- **Examine fears** - Are you susceptible to scare tactics regarding certain threats? Dissect why these frighten you and whether feelings align with facts.

Knowing your own weaknesses allows you to account for them rather than being exploited subconsciously. Work to overcome biases through exposure, education, and maintaining vigilance.

Balancing Emotions with Logic

Propaganda manipulates emotions like fear and anger to override rational thinking. Regain control through:

- **Recognizing agitation** - When you notice provocative content producing strong feelings, pause until the immediate intensity passes before reacting.

- **Labeling techniques** - Identify the specific tactics used to stoke emotions - this engages logic to counteract visceral reactions.

- **Seeking facts** - Before spreading anger-fueled messages, fact-check key claims to ensure truth aligns with feelings. Feeling riled up doesn't make claims accurate.

- **Prioritizing understanding** - In conflicts, make good faith efforts to grasp opponents' motivations and fears before attacking them. Channels outrage into empathy.

- **Allowing nuance** - Train yourself to find complexity rather than categorizing people or issues into boxes like "good/bad" or "ally/enemy."

Propaganda-proof minds balance emotion with analysis before taking actions that can't be undone.

Conquering Confirmation Bias

Confirmation bias leads us to reflexively accept claims that confirm pre-existing beliefs while rejecting contrasting information. Outsmart it by:

- **Reading opposing views directly** - Don't just learn about "the other side" through your own team's filter. Listen to their case in their own words.

- **Questioning agreeable claims** - Treat claims that validate your beliefs as rigorously as you would ones that conflict with them. Demand equal evidence.

- **Challenging sacred cows** - Don't let any beliefs or stances become immune to questioning. Entertain good faith critiques of your own side.

- **Posing the question**, "What if I am wrong?" entails a thoughtful examination of contrasting perspectives and visualizing how you would react if you discovered your error. Stubbornness frequently stems from a sense of pride.

- **Changing your mind** - View evolving your beliefs based on new evidence as strength, not weakness. Blind consistency in the face of contradictions is ignorance.

Leave no assumptions unchallenged. Make lifelong learning and intellectual flexibility priorities over clinging to ego and dogmas. An open yet critical mind immunizes against manipulation.

Avoiding Demagogic Rallies

Mass gatherings aimed at riling up fervor for a political leader, ideology, or cause are fertile ground for emotional manipulation. Certain environments are better avoided if you aim to resist propaganda's influence:

- **Charismatic speakers feeding off crowds** - Skeptically examine flawed logic and dishonest claims rather than getting swept up in herd enthusiasm.

- **Demonizing scapegoats** - Resist dehumanizing entire groups based on the actions of individuals. Tribal hatred of "the other" breeds conformity and blind allegiance.

- **Chanting conformist slogans** - Don't let peer pressure sway you into actions you may later regret like intimidating opponents.

- **Reinforcing isolation** - Wariness of fellow citizens outside the rally bubble undermines civic trust and divides communities. Seek unifying understanding.

- **Enforcing loyalty pledges** - No political leader merits unquestioning devotion; preserve moral autonomy. Beware demands to prove allegiance.

While thrilling, mass hyperemotional events undermine individual reasoning in ways that serve propagandists. Protect your autonomy.

Strengthening Media Literacy

Media literacy education arms citizens with knowledge to overcome propaganda influences. Learn to:

- **Detect misinformation** - Hone skills for fact-checking claims, analyzing sources, and recognizing manipulation techniques.

- **Evaluate media credibility** - Understand markers that distinguish quality journalism and ethical content creators.

- **Consider economic forces** - Recognize how profit incentives and business models shape media, including "engagement"-driven social platforms.

- **Examine political biases** - Perceive how partisan leanings across outlets result in selective or misleading coverage serving specific agendas.

- **Question information sources** - Develop awareness around where you get news and why those channels could skew perception.

Media literate citizens are propaganda-proof. Advocate for improved education to inoculate society.

The strategies in this chapter empower individuals to withstand propaganda's manipulations by strengthening mental habits. But collective action is also required against organized disinformation. Next, we'll examine how communities can come together to constructively respond.

Chapter 6: Combating Propaganda in Your Community

The critical thinking tools we've built form crucial individual defenses against propaganda. But since disinformation also corrodes public discourse and social cohesion at scale, collective countermeasures are needed. This chapter explores constructive grassroots responses citizens can pursue in their local communities.

Propaganda is only truly defeated through proactive efforts to spread truthful counter-narratives, inoculate society against manipulation, and demand reforms. Doing so not only improves resilience, but brings citizens together around shared facts and solutions.

1. Starting Local Conversations

Opening frank face-to-face conversations in your community combats isolation and mistrust bred by propaganda. Try hosting:

Non-partisan discussion groups - Convene across lines of division to build empathy and realize shared concerns. Set ground rules requiring respectful listening to counter hostility.

Classes/workshops on media literacy - Teach critical analysis of claims and responsible sharing. Equip citizens with knowledge to debunk falsehoods.

Support groups for ex-propaganda targets - Those indoctrinated into extremist ideologies need help safely transitioning out. Provide guidance in a judgement-free space.

Community screenings of relevant documentaries - Follow showings with moderated discussions connecting themes to local issues. Film inspires reflection.

Crowdsourced propaganda tracking - Gather examples of disinformation circulating locally to understand toxins poisoning your community's conversation.

Face-to-face connections foster mutual understanding that combats "us vs. them" divides. Start small through leading groups or just talking to neighbors.

2. Building Digital Media Literacy

Online outreach can also help local communities detect and counter falsehoods. Try:

Fact-checking viral posts - Create shareable graphics, videos, or posts identifying local disinformation with added facts and reporting.

Captioning misleading memes - Add factual context below popular unreliable memes to influence perceptions before sharing.

Writing letters to local media - Publish op-eds and letters urging greater responsibility and accuracy in local reporting.

Debunking through art - In creative communities, subvert propaganda through catchy songs, comedy, cartoons, ads etc conveying truth.

Creating research guides - Equip fellow citizens with lists of fact-checking sites, academic references, and balanced local reporting on key issues.

Using online forums - On community pages, politely point out and discuss disinformation posted, providing facts.

Digital literacy initiatives bring truth to citizens immersed in propaganda online.

3. Petitioning for Reforms

Change also requires demanding reforms from social media platforms, advertisers, and traditional media to reduce systemic propaganda incentives:

Write elected representatives - Lobby Congress to address Section 230 immunity and propose solutions like disclosure requirements.

Protest advertisers - Organize boycotts and pressure companies sponsoring partisan outlets spreading misinformation.

Submit commentary - Send local newspapers opinion columns urging solutions like transparency in ownership and sources.

Start online petitions - Campaign sites like Change.org enable petitioning leaders for anti-propaganda policies.

Form watchdog groups - Organize grassroots groups that document and publicly expose local disinformation.

Channel outrage at propagandists into constructive policy advocacy. Bottom-up pressure gets results.

4. Promoting High-Quality Journalism

Supporting journalists pursuing truth in the face of propaganda is vital civic duty. You can:

Subscribe and donate - Fund subscriptions to trustworthy local and national outlets. Also donate to non-profits like ProPublica doing investigative journalism.

Amplify reliable reporting - Follow and share vetted local reporters telling overlooked, inconvenient truths without bias.

Advocate for media reforms - Urge changes like increased public funding for news and rules on media consolidation.

Demand editorial independence - When coverage appears compromised by business interests, write editors urging separation.

Submit locally-focused story ideas - Send reporters tips on issues in need of investigation in your community.

Thank journalists - Recognize reporters who exemplify ethical standards with letters and awards.

Truth-focused journalism shields communities from propaganda. Readers must provide moral and financial support.

5. Monitoring Information Sources

To clean up propaganda plaguing local conversations, track where it originates:

Trace claims to root spreaders - When viral dubious stories appear locally, dig to uncover and expose propagandists responsible.

Map social network ties - Visually chart how local political figures, pages, and groups share and amplify the same propaganda sources.

Identify outside influencers - Note accounts stoking local tensions while lacking any real ties to community.

Check event sponsors - Investigate who funds local rallies and speeches spreading disinformation.

Follow the money - Which foreign and domestic entities finance media outlets popular with local groups spreading propaganda?

Understanding propaganda ecosystems informs strategic responses. Make transparency and accountability goals.

6. Inoculating Against Hate

A vital defense against propaganda is inoculating citizens against hateful ideologies before indoctrination occurs. Methods include:

Anti-extremism education - Equip teachers and parents with resources to discuss and debunk radicalizing messages targeting youth.

Media literacy training - Teach critical thinking and fact verification as mandatory skills for the digital age in schools.

alternative Programming - Support activities giving isolated youth a sense of purpose and community beyond radicals promising meaning.

Intervention hotlines - Create local tip lines for families, students etc to report concerns over extremist rhetoric, before it's too late.

Reintegration help - Develop resources to safely help former extremists transition out of hate groups and repair community relationships.

Informed and mindful citizens are less vulnerable to propaganda. Start by safeguarding those who are most at risk.

7. Building Community Resilience

Finally, fostering strong communal ties fortifies societies against propaganda seeking to divide people against each other. Try:

Organizing volunteer projects - Bring diverse locals together through service projects and community improvement initiatives.

Promoting cultural events - Sponsor inclusive cultural activities like potlucks, music, and sports that build familiarity across groups.

Holding interfaith activities - Arrange joint forums where local religious leaders can highlight universal values.

Supporting dialogue programs - Advocate for school curricula and workshops facilitating constructive discussions on difficult issues.

Sharing more local stories - Collect and circulate tales that highlight common ground and portray shared struggles.

Framed competently, a town is inoculated against hate. Social cohesion arises from grassroots community-building, not top-down platform policies. You have the power to lead this movement.

Chapter 7: Protecting Democracy in the Information Age

The strategies we've covered equip citizens to detect and counter propaganda as individuals and communities. But lasting solutions require addressing misinformation's systemic causes through policy reforms, technological innovation, and improved education.

This chapter explores overarching approaches society must pursue to rein in propaganda and preserve inclusive democracy in the digital age. We face an epic challenge, but pragmatic steps can reclaim truth.

Reforming Social Media

Social media platforms have fundamentally reshaped information flows by optimizing for engagement over veracity. Policy reforms and settlements imposing transparency, accountability, and oversight would help correct distortions.

Public Interest Regulation

Federal regulatory agencies could be empowered to impose standards on social media in the public's interest, balancing free speech with safety. Potential policy directions include:

- Requiring transparency around business practices, algorithms, data collection, and content moderation policies.

- Prohibiting designed addiction via continual notifications and infinite scrolls that erode user agency.

- Banning microtargeted advertising based on private psychological profiles.

- Mandating consistent identity verification to eliminate inauthentic accounts and bots.

- Charging platforms legally as publishers if they recommend content via algorithms.

- Creating civil liabilities for platforms that amplify illegal speech or permit harassment.

- Appointing external bodies to conduct human rights impact assessments and propose reforms.

- Establishing dedicated regulatory agencies to draft and oversee social media rules protecting democracy and privacy.

Anti-Trust Action

Breaking up social media giants could reduce centralized control and refocus firms on serving users over advertisers. Spinning off companies' acquisitions like Instagram and WhatsApp could spur more alternatives. Interoperability mandates enabling cross-platform sharing could also decentralize networks and data.

Section 230 Reform

This law currently immunizes platforms from liability for user-generated illegal content and misconduct. Refining Section 230 to hold firms accountable for moderation decisions could pressure improvements. But reforms must avoid over-censorship or vagueness in defining unlawful content.

Transparency Requirements

Laws requiring social media companies to regularly disclose data and analysis on issues like bot activity, algorithmic amplification effects, impressions by geography and demographics, and content moderation actions would enable oversight. Firms may then be pressured by media coverage and researchers' findings to mitigate identified harms.

Self-Regulation

Some argue the industry should voluntarily self-impose standards through an association developing best practices for transparency, ethics, privacy, and content policies. But skepticism surrounds whether competitive pressures would permit meaningful cooperation. Still, articulating norms could establish public benchmarks to evaluate companies against.

Financial Penalties

Multi-billion dollar fines by the FTC and European regulators for breaches have successfully pressured reforms around privacy at Facebook and other tech giants. Continued steep penalties contingent on progress in content and data policies could incentivize companies to rethink entire business models.

Taxation

Levying special taxes on microtargeted ads or collecting user data could deter surveillance capitalism powering disinformation. New revenues could also fund counter-propaganda education and journalism. But avoid overburdening smaller firms.

Overall, a balanced but assertive combination of antitrust enforcement, financial penalties, transparency laws, and threat of regulation could push platforms to finally make user well-being - not endless growth at any cost - central.

Rethinking Social Incentives

Changes to underlying incentives and structures driving social platforms' optimization of engagement over truth are also crucial.

Prioritizing Quality Interactions

A core solution lies in shifting platforms' metrics for success - awarded "likes" and comments - from quantity to QUALITY of engagement between users. Platforms should develop robust ways to assess whether exchanges represent meaningful dialogue versus angry polarization. Highly-rated interactions would then be recommended over base exchanges cynically designed to enrage.

Community-Driven Moderation

Rather than centralized policies, community-specific moderation approaches could grant users agency over their own interactions. Smaller groups could self-determine norms and mete out penalties like temporary bans. Moderation would then reflect diverse cultural values.

Non-Profit Alternatives

Today's dominant commercial social networks monetize outrage. But non-profit platforms devoted to healthy connections over addiction could realign incentives. Peer-to-peer networks owned by local collectives rather than companies are one option. Diaspora, Mastadon, and Scuttlebutt have pioneered early examples worth expanding.

Public Funding Models

Rather than ad revenue, platforms could receive public funding while incorporating community representation and free expression protections on their boards, becoming a "social media public option." Such reforms could constructively meet needs for connection without undermining citizenship.

Promoting Quality Journalism

Propaganda flourishes when quality journalism declines. But the digital age has decimated conventional reporting models. Steps must be taken to fund public interest news and reform distorted media incentives:

Public Media Funding

Direct government funding for public media like NPR, PBS, and the BBC improves journalism by shielding it from commercial pressures to chase clicks and outrage. Expanding funds for such outlets would help local news and investigative reporting overcome industry struggles.

R&D for New Models

Grants could support research into news business models - like reader revenue and low-profit corporate forms - designed around communities needs rather than endless growth. Philanthropic capital could also fund experimental journalism startups pursuing reforms. Lessons can inform industry shifts.

Platform Compensation

Proposed "link taxes" that force platforms like Facebook to pay news outlets for using their content could fund struggling journalism. But risks around stifling digital sharing must be navigated. An Australian approach requiring negotiation seems balanced.

Non-Profit Support

Policies like making nonprofit news organizations tax-exempt and allowing tax-deductible public donations could assist investigative reporting. Measures to simplify operation requirements for nonprofit media versus for-profits may also enable growth.

Accountability Journalism

Groups like ProPublica that focus exclusively on large-scale investigative projects exposing misinformation sources serve a vital role deserving expanded funding. Their work signals journalism's highest purpose and demonstrates public demand.

Public Data Access

Governments could strengthen journalism's capacity for accountability by sharing data sets online for analysis around issues like crime statistics or pollution. Information asymmetries otherwise allow disinformation to thrive.

A mixture of funding, incentives changes, and policy reforms can rejuvenate journalism as democracy's safeguard against propaganda in the 21st century.

Improving Civic Education

Educational initiatives to strengthen citizens' resistance to propaganda and grasp of democratic values are essential long-term solutions. This requires:

Mandatory Media Literacy

Schools K through 12 must teach core skills like sourcing and fact-checking information, identifying propaganda techniques, avoiding echo chambers, and analyzing credibility. These digital media literacy skills build defenses against manipulation.

News Analysis Training

Secondary schools should incorporate current event discussions analyzing media portrayals, biases, inconsistencies, and framing effects. Teaching students to critically deconstruct news narratives coming at them daily builds skepticism.

Anti-Radicalization Education

Inoculating youth against extremist ideologies requires explaining totalitarian tactics and helping students feel agency responding to propaganda seeking to radicalize them towards violence. Emphasize moral autonomy.

Confronting Misinformation Early

Elementary educators must get comfortable discussing even controversial issues in kids' lives like public health or political propaganda spreading on social media before malicious actors fill the void. Establish a prosocial baseline.

Prioritizing Civics

Reviving high quality civics curriculum centered on democratic principles, civil discourse, recognizing propaganda, navigating media, and modeling tolerance fosters responsible digital citizenship. Required civics classes should get equal attention to core STEM fields.

Community Media Literacy Programs

Libraries, religious institutions, community centers, and local governments can also provide adult education around analyzing propaganda, fact-checking techniques, responsible social media use, and supporting local accountability journalism.

Equipping society with the knowledge citizens require for self-governance in the 21st century will determine the fate of inclusive democracy. We must seize this challenge.

Harnessing Technology for Truth

Advances in ethical AI, forensic media analysis, and decentralized networks could also combat propaganda by empowering citizens:

Automated Fact-Checking

AI tools capable of fact-checking claims at scale during debates by comparing statements in real time to databases of truthful information could assist viewers in judging truthfulness. Natural language processing able to rate the factual accuracy of articles also holds promise.

Deepfake Detection

Machine learning algorithms trained to identify manipulated images, videos, and audio could help contain falsified media. Fake content leaves digital traces detectible by forensic analysis. To stay ahead of disinformation, such detection tools must constantly evolve as creation techniques advance.

Bot Identification

Bots amplifying propaganda could be countered by automated systems identifying and flagging inauthentic accounts to platforms based on patterns like non-human posting frequencies, stolen photos, and coordinated swarming attacks. This would enable removal before manipulation spreads.

Crowdsourced Propaganda Tracking

Secure online dashboards empowering citizens to anonymously submit examples of propaganda encountered across social media, advertisements, events, etc to database archives would help researchers analyze tactics. Aggregated data reveals coordinated influence campaigns.

Decentralized Networks

Blockchain-based social networks and platforms offer less centralized control over content, diminishing power for centralized manipulation and censorship. User-run content rating systems relying on consensus could improve stability and trust long-term.

Technology poses challenges today, but imagined responsibly it can tip the scales towards truth - if we demand it.

Taxing Disinformation

Legislative approaches to make propaganda financially unviable could include:

Taxing Targeted Ads

Levying special taxes on microtargeted ads based on individual data profiles could deter corporate and political entities from exploiting personal weaknesses for manipulation.

Taxing Bot Activity

Penalizing platforms that fail to curb large-scale inauthentic bot accounts which amplify propaganda could pressure reforms. Make polluting the information ecosystem costly.

Taxing Fake News Sources

Sites demonstrably publishing false propaganda masquerading as news could face penalties or denial of business tax deductions. But protections for satire must be codified.

Tax Breaks for Journalism

Special tax credits and deductions could assist legitimate journalistic outlets, especially small local newsrooms, allowing survival in the face of propaganda sources unburdened by truth-seeking.

Funding Counter-Propaganda

Taxes on ads and platforms could supply grants for non-profits combating propaganda through fact-checking, media literacy programs, and counter-narrative campaigns. Fines for disinformation could also fund solutions.

Global Cooperation

As propaganda transcends borders online, multinational cooperation is imperative to avoid whack-a-mole effects:

Information Sharing

Intelligence agencies and cybersecurity researchers in democracies must coordinate early threat detection, sharing tactics of state-sponsored troll farms and botnets attempting to interfere in elections and seed chaos. Mobilizing collective defenses quicker can thwart globalized propaganda.

Exporting Media Literacy

Nations globally must collaborate in developing media literacy educational approaches and tools that can spread to classrooms in diverse cultural contexts. Shared knowledge will fortify democratic citizenship worldwide.

International Norm Setting

Democratic countries must jointly establish norms condemning state propaganda targeting of foreign populations online and work to bring the world behind these principles. Global opinion aligned on basic violations increases pressure for change.

Prosecuting Online Radicalization

Nations should coordinate policy approaches regarding propaganda and recruitment content from violent extremist groups that operates across borders online. Right to free expression must be balanced with combating radicalization to violence.

Harnessing Cross-Border Fact Checkers

Platforms should assist collaborative international fact-checking networks capable of debunking viral misinformation in diverse languages and cultural contexts. Accuracy should supersede borders.

Through formal institutions and civil society cooperation, global partnerships can contain forces seeking to divide humanity and undermine democracy worldwide. Truth knows no nations.

Conclusion: Reclaiming Reality

In an era where technology allows reality itself to be questioned on a global scale, defending inclusive, evidence-based societies is humanity's urgent duty. Propaganda, misinformation, and denialism cannot be tolerated to reign unchecked.

But through ethical reforms, education, focused innovation, and cooperation we can fortify democratic citizenship for the digital age. Societies centered on wisdom and compassion can yet triumph over those founded on profit and manipulation.

We ordinary citizens must awaken to reclaim agency over our own mindsets, conversations, and communities. The disinformation dance can be mastered through knowledge, vigilance, and moral courage. But the first steps begin inside each of us.

I hope this book has equipped you to participate in that dance with eyes open, mind skeptical, heart compassionate, and voice loud. The fate of truth depends on what we collectively demand and build going forward. My faith rests in our shared humanity and reason.

Now let's get to work - having conversations, organizing grassroots efforts, contacting leaders, and voting to defend facts and inclusive democracy against the polluting tides of propaganda.

We cock an ear towards those speaking truths, hold accountable those deceiving humanity, and keep walking steadily on the long road towards justice. The darkness of dishonesty cannot withstand the light of engaged citizens.

Ours is an epic struggle, make no mistake. But throughout history, we find ordinary people rising up against tyranny, zealotry, and hatred to build a more enlightened world brick by brick. That legacy lives within us.

In unity, clarity, and hope we must write the next chapter. I believe we will choose the path of truth and reason over lies and fearmongering. The pen is in our hands - as is the future.

Now let us dance forthrightly and take back our power. The truth shall set us free.

About the Author

Monday Farouq has dedicated his life's work to understanding the intricacies of the human mind and spirit. As a psychologist and rehabilitation specialist, he has spent decades assisting individuals in improving their mental health, overcoming personal challenges, and enhancing their quality of life.

Yet in recent years, Dr. Farouq became increasingly concerned by broader societal trends that seemed to be negatively impacting human psychology and social cohesion on a mass scale. The rapid proliferation of misinformation, conspiracy theories, and propaganda in the internet age alarmed him given his expertise in how such forces can destabilize individual psyches.

After witnessing first-hand how such disinformation radicalized citizens towards extremism, he felt morally compelled to raise awareness around this modern crisis. While his previous books focused on clinical practice, he pivoted to addressing the "mind viruses" infecting public conversations, which he saw as an existential threat to inclusive democracy if left unchecked.

Despite the darkness, Dr. Farouq remains an optimist at heart. He firmly believes that by empowering ordinary citizens with knowledge and compassion, humanity can counter the "disinformation dance" threatening reason and truth. This book represents his sincere attempt to illuminate problems but also provide pragmatic solutions.

When he is not writing, Dr. Farouq enjoys dining with friends, attending musical concerts, interacting with nature, and playing strategy games that stimulate the mind. He also volunteers at a community center offering mental health support and media literacy classes for at-risk youth. He aims to practice the same empathy and understanding with all people that his work promotes.

Dr. Farouq invites you to join him on this urgent mission to fortify citizenship and reclaim our information ecosystem from propaganda. He sees this book as the start of a movement, not the end. There is much work ahead, but he has faith we will succeed together.

www.ingramcontent.com/pod-product-compliance
Lightning Source LLC
Chambersburg PA
CBHW071106260726
48661CB00006B/2503